The
MYSTICAL
SURRENDER

The
MYSTICAL
SURRENDER

Giving In

Translated by
Carla R. Mancari

Celestial Literary Group

To
Mary Carpenter,
Called

The contents of this book are not meant to take the place of qualified medical professionals or therapists. There is no expressed or implied guarantee as to the effects of the suggestions given or the liability taken.

CONTENTS

ACKNOWLEDGMENTS

Thanks to Mary Carpenter, who reviewed and edited a difficult work. Accomplishing this work would not have been possible without her interest in it.

I am grateful for the revelation of the Christ Consciousness Meditation and the inspiration of the Holy Spirit in the name of Jesus Christ. Without them, this work would not be possible.

INTRODUCTION

Mystical Surrender: Giving In is written to give a definitive, precise Christian understanding of the spiritual journey. It offers a view of what it means to surrender to Jesus Christ. The writer intends to caution *and* encourage you to surrender and follow Jesus Christ.

There is no attempt to soft-peddle your spiritual journey. However, its fruits are its own reward. It is you who must ultimately decide to walk in *His* footprints.

Included is a review of The Spiritual Center, The Christ Consciousness Meditation, and Exercises. All are to support and allow your surrender and spiritual journey to be as smooth as possible. Jesus is guiding you every step of the way.

All Bible Scripture verses are from the King James Version, London: Syndics of Cambridge University Press, Bentley

House, American Branch, New York, printed in Great Britain.

1

GIVING IN

Giving in to Jesus is accepting the invitation. As it is written in Scripture, Jesus is always inviting you to follow Him every moment of your life. It is an invitation to share with Him the gifts and nature of God. *"And he saith unto them, Follow me, and I will make you fishers of men"* (Matthew 4: 19).

Jesus never withdraws the invitation. It is an open-ended invitation that allows you to give in and follow Him in your own time and at your own pace. Jesus invites you and then patiently awaits your arrival.

Jesus never pushes. He invites and is available. It is an invitation; you need not know the way. Just allow yourself to give in, and Jesus will show you the way. When you are ready, the inner door opens wide. Step inside.

Jesus has instructed you to follow His example, His way, and His teachings. He has left a trail to follow. It is not difficult to find. It awaits your footsteps. *"For even hereunto were ye called: because Christ also suffered for us, leaving us an example, that ye should follow his steps"* (I Peter 2: 21).

You are invited to give in, surrender, and return to your spirituality. The way home lies within you. The candies of this world are bittersweet; they will not last, nor can they ever fill you as Christ can.

Accept the invitation, and through the activity of the Holy Spirit in the name of Jesus Christ, the way home will be a light one. *"Come unto me, all ye that labour and are heavy laden, and I will give you rest"* (Matthew 11:28).

Jesus promises to lead. Accept His invitation, "Follow Me." You are invited to share all that God has and all that God is. Accept the invitation to follow Him, and be guided to a spiritual feast of the truth in the Oneness of the Christ Consciousness. Give in, surrender to Jesus.

2

**THE
CHRIST
CONSCIOUSNESS**

The Christ Consciousness (Father, the One) is the finest vibrating energy. Within the Christ Consciousness are many individual states of consciousness. Until the realization of the finest, purest Christ Consciousness state, there is a consciousness of an individual self-identity.

When realizing the finest, purest Christ Consciousness state, there is no individual self-identity, no person. There is just *be-ing* the Christ Consciousness. You cannot remain in this realized state while your individual expression of it continues to exist on the earth plane of opposites. You have merely changed the vibratory frequency from the individual expression to the finest, purest Christ Consciousness state.

Once you surrender and the finest, purest Christ Consciousness state is realized, its frequency again descends as an individual expression, you. The realization remains with you because realizations are your nature. The Christ Consciousness manifests as an individual expression of the Christ Consciousness – not in a relationship with or separate from it.

It is when the Christ Consciousness descends as an individual expression, and the mind state of consciousness rises as "I, Me," that there is this false sense of a separate self. It is a false sense of a separate self that has no existence in the Christ Consciousness of your spirituality. Whether you are working with an inner teacher, Jesus, or an outer teacher, you are working with the same Christ Consciousness. Jesus Christ, an outer teacher, and *your* consciousness; *all* three (individual expressions) are manifesting as the Christ Consciousness.

Always the Christ Consciousness is expressing as individual expressions of consciousness. The individual expressions may surrender and ascend to their realized conscious awareness of the finest Christ Consciousness state. The difference is the realization of it. When in a conscious mystical surrender, through a strait gate and narrow way, the finest Christ Consciousness state may be realized.

3

THE
STRAIT GATE
And
NARROW WAY

Strait is the gate, and narrow is the way between the resting mind and your sacred Spiritual Center (Chapter 13). It is the way that may directly lead to the awareness of Christ Consciousness. *"Then said Jesus unto them again, Verily, verily, I say unto you, I am the door of the sheep"* (John 10: 7).

As a truth seeker, strait is the gate and narrow is the way that Jesus instructs you to follow, *"Because strait is the gate, and narrow is the way, which leadeth unto life, and few there be that find it"* (Matthew 7: 14).

It may be the most difficult to find; however, once surrendered, it is most available with the help and guidance of Jesus Christ. *"That thy way may be known upon earth, thy saving health among all nations"* (Psalm 67: 2).

When you intentionally surrender and begin practicing the silent Christ Consciousness Meditation (Chapter 15), you are taking the strait gate and narrow way; you have found it. If the strait gate and narrow way are difficult for you to follow, be in constant remembrance, *"I can of mine own self do nothing ..."* (John 5: 30).

A realized conscious awareness of this one Scripture teaching will take you to the strait gate and narrow way. It will bring you into a humble spirit. It may help you to maintain your meditation practice.

The strait gate and narrow way don't accept weak attempts. It is the way that requires all that you are and all that you can be. Trust that the bumps on the way will smooth out as you wear them down. Every moment you practice the Christ Consciousness Meditation, it may help to smooth out a rough spot.

There is no room for experimentation or compromise along the way. There is never an allowance for wavering from the known truth. It requires complete surrender, devotion, obedience, and earnest determination. However, it allows for time out and rests as it moves you on, either slowly or rapidly, according to your devotional determination.

At times, Jesus walks slowly, allowing you to catch up; and at other times, He stops to wait for you. *"In all thy ways acknowledge him, and he shall direct thy paths"* (Proverbs 3: 6).

The strait gate and narrow way has no bends or slants. It goes in one direction at all times, from the resting mind to your sacred Spiritual Center, and looking back or around may cause stumbling or possibly falling onto another way—a way that appears easier to travel because the gate is wide and the way broad. Be not deceived*: "Enter ye in at the strait gate: for wide is the gate, and broad is the way, that leadeth to destruction, and many there be which go in thereat"* (Matthew 7: 13).

The strait gate and narrow way takes you home to the awareness of the

Christ Consciousness within your Spiritual Center, and because you have done all in *His* name, Jesus awaits your arrival. Place your total dependence and trust in Jesus Christ. Jesus will lead the way.

4

TRUST
IN
JESUS CHRIST

Trust in Jesus Christ is the mystical surrendering to the Will of God in all your ways; *"not my will, but thine be done "* (Luke 22: 42).

When you begin a spiritual journey, you do so with trust in the inner guidance of Jesus Christ. You place your faith in Jesus Christ for the sheer joy of realizing your spirituality and the activity of the Holy Spirit. Any other benefits are secondary. *"Cease ye from man, whose breath is in his nostrils: for wherein is he to be accounted of?"* (Isaiah 2: 22).

Turning to Jesus Christ strengthens and accelerates your individual expression of vibrating energy consciousness. When your mental energies focus on the things of this world, they may seem real, and you may easily drift into a world of illusion. *"Those who find their life will lose it, and those who lose their life for my sake will find it"* (Matthew 10: 39).

In times of chaos and confusion, you need to trust in Jesus Christ. With fidelity to your mystical surrender, trust in Jesus Christ is gradually fortified. *"No weapon that is formed against thee shall prosper, and every tongue that shall rise against thee in judgment thou shalt condemn. This is the heritage of the servants of the LORD, and their righteousness is of me, saith the LORD"* (Isaiah 54:17).

Overcoming, under all circumstances, the temptation to become distracted by the things of this world is possible when your trust remains in Jesus Christ. The truth of your fulfillment is in Jesus Christ, and all other attractions may cease to sway you and draw you from your surrender. *"It is better to trust in the LORD than to put confidence in princes"* (Psalm 118:9).

When you surrender, you may realize that Jesus Christ is real and meets all your needs, regardless of appearances.

"And Jesus said unto them, I am the bread of life." (John 6:35).

Be steadfast, and trust in Jesus Christ's Holy Spirit, the spirit of truth. Such trust does not go unrewarded. *"THEY that trust in the LORD shall be as Mount Zion, which cannot be moved, but abideth"* (Psalm 125:1).

5

THE
HOLY SPIRIT
SPIRIT OF TRUTH

The Holy Spirit, in the name of Jesus Christ, is the spirit of truth that speaks on behalf of truth hidden from all ages. It teaches what lies beyond words and images. There is never a time when the Holy Spirit in the name of Jesus Christ is not descending, coming.

There is no withholding of the spirit of truth from any individual—the "when" is at the receiver's discretion. The minute there is the slightest inclination to surrender to Jesus Christ, the Holy Spirit of truth descends and proceeds to lead and teach. It is never withholding.

Jesus' Holy Spirit is poured out upon all creation without discrimination or partiality. All that is Jesus is His to give. When you are ready to surrender, the Holy Spirit, in the name of Jesus Christ, teaches simply, deliberately, and without delay, or disguise, in accordance with your surrender.

Preparation is important. Physical, emotional, and spiritual readiness are prerequisites for your surrender. A listening posture is essential. The discipline of interior silence is a seedbed for the awareness of the Holy Spirit's voice. The Holy Spirit speaks in silence. Cultivate interior silence with the help of the Listening-in Exercise (Chapter 16).

The Holy Spirit is the teaching advocate and comforter who will reveal the Son in the Father. God the Father, Son, or Holy Spirit may at times reveal truth, and when doing so, all participate while remaining silent. The most appropriate for communication is the Holy Spirit of truth.

There is no hierarchy in God. There is only equality, oneness, and love. No competition, no greater than, or lesser than. No higher than, or lower than, just the one at any and every moment expressing, teaching, loving, creating, sustaining, and sanctifying all that is itself forever to those who would surrender.

That for which you wait is already present. Always has been and always will be. When you realize reality, any sense of the past or future ceases. Until you understand this, it is common to "sense" a future. When you realize the "future" as the present, the "things to come" will have arrived, never to depart.

The glory of God is the glory of the Son. Jesus has glorified God and given you that same glory, which is also God's glory. All that the Father has is Jesus', and the Holy Spirit of truth takes what is Jesus' and declares it to you.

All are the One Christ Consciousness expressing as the many. Surrender in humility, a humble spirit in the Oneness, and live that glory that Jesus shares. *"And the glory which thou gavest me I have given them; that they may be one, even as we are one"* (John 17: 22).

6

**HUMILITY
A
HUMBLE SPIRIT**

Humility, a humble spirit, is when Jesus surrendered and said, "Yes" to the Father, "Thy will be done." Jesus consented to suffer torturous persecution and crucifixion. He allowed man to strip Him of His human dignity. He was the ultimate in humility and a humble spirit. *"Humble yourselves therefore under the mighty hand of God, that he may exalt you in due time"* (I Peter 5:6).

Jesus was aware there was no personal sense of an "I" to defend. In this world, you are always on the defensive. You are always in a state of readiness to defend, protect, or justify your beliefs and actions.

Humility is within your God-essence. It is waiting to surface from beneath this world of false concepts. With the slightest crack of your worldly armor, humility and a humble spirit may be revealed from within you. Usually, it rises during a humiliating experience when you "know" you are right.

Once realized, humility is ever ready to express itself gently.

Humility, a humble spirit, is not easily realized. You may be approaching your silent meditation practice and temptations that arise in your daily life with the attitude, "I can do this." The misconception is that there is a personal "I" who must or can do anything. *"I am the vine, ye are the branches: He that abideth in me, and I in him, the same bringeth forth much fruit: for without me ye can do nothing"* (John 15:5).

The realization that may move you into humility, a humble spirit, is, "Of myself I do nothing." Therefore, there is no "self, I" to defend or protect. It is in realizing "Of myself, I do nothing" that may bring you to the doorstep of humility, a humble spirit.

It may give you the permission and freedom to reach within for whatever the need is at the moment—and that includes humility, a humble spirit. *"If ye abide in me, and my words abide in you, ye shall ask what ye will, and it shall be done unto you"* (John 15: 7).

You may find humility, a humble spirit, challenging to realize and to flow from every pore of your being until you, too, realize, as Jesus did, who is doing the works. *"Believest thou not that I am in the Father, and the Father in me? The words that I speak unto you I speak not of myself: but the Father that dwelleth in me, he doeth the works"* (John 14: 10).

It may be difficult for you because humility is a quality of being that does not seek anything and gives up the intentional outer show when fame, honors, and platitudes are presented. *"Whosoever therefore shall humble himself as this little child, the same is greatest in the kingdom of heaven"* (Matthew 18: 4).

Pride may be a hindrance to admitting humility. *"Pride goeth before destruction, and a haughty spirit before a fall. Better it is to be of a humble spirit with the lowly than to divide the spoil with the proud"* (Proverbs 16: 18-19).

Humility, humble in spirit, is not necessarily a soft voice or an embarrassed smile when others praise you. It is not a display of false modesty. You are asked to be humble but firm in all you may do through the Holy Spirit in the name of Jesus Christ. Humility, humble in spirit, holds on to nothing, realizing there is never anything to hold on to because, in the kingdom of God, all needs are already met. You come as a child of God, open and trusting.

In humility, you are aware there is nothing out there that can be added to your already complete spirituality. You are aware that all is here for your use, and, in reality, there is no ownership. You cannot own the temporary, which is relative to the earth's plane of opposites.

It may be possible for you to be a truth student of long standing and still struggle with the humility of your Christ

Consciousness realization. The lack of obedience and discipline may prevent the awareness of true humility. In humility, as a humble spirit, you surrender to the Christ of your being without question and believe beyond any doubt in the path you have chosen. Then the inner and outer help necessary for continued guidance in your progress on the spiritual walk is received.

When the willful pride of your stubbornness is awash in humility, you accept that which is asked of you. Throughout all your trials, temptations, and struggles on this walk, Jesus Christ gives you help and transmits it to you in ways you may not always understand. Whatever the need, there is someone or something to assist. It is always you who must accept the way Jesus may select to assist you. *"Humble yourselves in the sight of the Lord, and he shall lift you up"* (James 4: 10).

While you are still in this world and doing the service given to you, it is with humility, a humble spirit, that you may overcome attachment to the rising appearances of this world. Humility brings you before the Christ-awareness of your being. It asks for all that you are. It allows you to remain in this world but not be of it. With discipline and obedience, and a humble spirit, your silent Christ Consciousness Meditation practice (Chapter 15) may be filled, allowing you to grow in the teachings of the Holy Spirit in the name of Jesus Christ.

Humility permits you to drop haughtiness and pridefulness and strips you bare of all pretenses. When, with free will, you surrender and are humble in spirit, you walk in humility, speak in humility, see in humility, touch in humility, and love in humility. You are the grace of God expressing God's will in humility, a humble spirit.

7

FREE WILL

Free will is the exercise of concentrated mental, vibrating energy applied to any wish, desire, or temptation that grabs your attention. Often referred to as "willpower," concentrated mental vibrating energy possesses extraordinary strength. It may accomplish difficult tasks when seeking to fulfill desires, overcoming temptations, or realizing the truth.

You have wishes, desires, and temptations. You don't necessarily fulfill most wishes and desires, nor do you succumb to all attractions. There are desires you plan to fulfill using free will. There are temptations you may need to use your free will to overcome, as Jesus did. *"Get thee behind me, Satan!"* (Luke 4: 8)

When you are ardently intent on fulfilling a wish or desire, or responding to a temptation, free will moves you to a plan of action. It helps to maintain your attention span until the desire is fulfilled or the temptation is overcome. Free will is the engine that drives the car. It takes you wherever it is you believe you want to go. However, you may find you do not want to be there once you have arrived. So, be careful what you wish for! *"For my thoughts are not your thoughts, neither are your ways my ways, saith the Lord"* (Isaiah 55: 8).

It is the strength of your belief, faith, and free will that may bring to fruition your wishes, desires, or plans. It is by sheer "willpower" that you may overcome adversities through the Holy Spirit in the name of Jesus Christ. Jesus gives you an example to follow. *"O my Father, if it be possible, let this cup pass from me: nevertheless not as I will, but as thou wilt"* (Matthew 26: 39).

As an aware, conscious spiritual being, you have the free will to choose to manifest desires and act or not. In progressively realizing the truth, you become aware that "nevertheless not my will, but thine be done" (Luke 22:42).

All that you are and ever will be is the nature of God. As you surrender, in this lifetime, you may realize the Oneness of your reality and the awareness that free will *is* divine will, God's will. *"Thy Kingdom come. Thy will be done in earth, as it is in heaven"* (Matthew 6: 10).

8

IN
THIS LIFETIME

In this lifetime, you have the opportunity to surrender to the Christ of your being and wake up to your reality. Like many students, you may struggle with the question, "Why this lifetime, why not before?" It was all of the "before" lifetimes that readied and prepared you for "*this* lifetime." Your readiness and preparedness were necessary for your mystical surrender, for you to begin the waking-up process in this lifetime. Your spiritual journey consists of many lifetimes. You did not just suddenly decide one day that you were going to surrender and wake up. No, many paths and many teachers along the way during your many lifetimes helped to bring you to *this* lifetime.

Fret no more about previous lifetimes. be aware that it is in "*this* lifetime" that you may surrender and wake up to your reality and dream walk no more. Jesus was obedient in His lifetime, and He made the necessary decision when indecision prevailed. He trusted that the Father was aware of His struggle. Jesus struggled with the choice He was given. He struggled with its difficulty. However, Jesus never questioned the direction of His path or the Father's motives, nor did He doubt what was asked of Him. *"And he went a little further, and fell on his face, and prayed, saying, O my Father, if it be possible, let this cup pass from me: nevertheless not as I will, but as thou wilt"* (Matthew 26:39).

Begin your spiritual journey without indecision or looking backward, and the path will be much smoother. *This* lifetime is the most important one. Surrender, do not waste it.

9

INDECISION

Indecision is a state of confused mental paralysis. Perpetual indecision is an abusive relationship that you have with yourself. *"Multitudes, multitudes in the valley of decision: for the day of the LORD is near in the valley of decision"* (Joel 3:14).

Surrendering to Jesus Christ on the spiritual path requires two prerequisites. Is it necessary? Will it contribute to spiritual growth? You are always in the "now," and it is in the "now" that you must decide to surrender. A tomorrow "now" may require a change, but "now" requires your decision.

Ultimately, "now" is when you must decide. How many "nows" have you struggled with that were indecisive? There may be unnecessary time and effort wasted on the notion, "Should I surrender, or shouldn't I?" "Is it right or wrong?"

The fear of making a mistake or not pleasing others may hold you in a paralytic mental state that torments your every thought. Stalling and continually repeating the same argument with the same old pros and cons may exact a tremendous toll on your physical, emotional, and spiritual well-being. Delaying your surrender to Jesus Christ interferes with your spiritual progress. The Lord does not decide for you. Refusal to act is a refusal to take responsibility for your own decision. You must choose to surrender. You must claim it. You must accept responsibility for it.

Inner or outer indecisive struggles are a sure sign that a change may be necessary. It may be time to break from the old, to let go, to give in, or to recognize that you are not in the place where you belong. It may not be easy. Easy is not what this journey is about. There may be a lifetime of fear of stepping out of the familiar and going to the edge of the unknown. It does require total and complete trust in your Lord. *"But I trusted in thee, O LORD: Thou art my God"* (Psalm 31: 14).

Your surrender on the earth's plane of opposites entertains change, and change is the one constant that you can count on. Your very existence on this earth plane invites change. *"Behold, I shew you a mystery; We shall not all sleep, but we shall all be changed"* (I Corinthians 15: 51).

A paralytic mind will break you. A committed, flexible fluid movement through this journey of surrender will set you free. *"O death, where is thy sting? O grave, where is thy victory?"* (I Corinthians 15: 55).

10

COMMITMENT

A commitment is what you make when you surrender and are a serious student on a spiritual journey. There are times on your spiritual journey when you may find it easy to abandon a commitment. It is not from lapse of memory but rather from rationalization. You may have many good excuses for not keeping your commitment to your surrender to your Lord, but not one good reason.

The one good reason for a wavering commitment is that it was never an inner commitment. An outer commitment comes from the mental realm. Thus, it can be rationalized away – into oblivion. An inner commitment does not let go because it is beyond the mental realm; hence, it cannot be justified anywhere. The outer commitment is always looking for a way out. Its sincerity is weak, to begin with, and therefore cannot sustain itself.

An inner commitment grows in strength and supports your spiritual practices. You may have a tendency to want to impress a teacher with your talk of commitment. But an inner commitment does not require words, for its actions speak louder than any outward show.

You may come to be aware that you are called to the extraordinary mystical surrender of your being that allows you to commit, bow your head, and bend your knees before the divine of your being. And when you rise again, you are immersed in the realization of this "I am" that you are, and there is no higher, no lower—only that which you are, always have been, and will be throughout all eternity. *"And God said to Moses, I AM THAT I AM ..."* (Exodus 3: 14).

11

CALLED

From the moment you surrender and seriously step onto the spiritual path, individuals, invitations, events, and places are drawn to your consideration. There is an inner call that manifests in some form or another. Living from the inner to the outer world allows you to hear clearly. When you are called, you respond appropriately. *"I press toward the mark for the prize of the high calling of God in Christ Jesus"* (Philippians 3: 14).

As you answer the call, Jesus Christ guides and places you exactly where you should be at all times. *"Thou shalt call, and I will answer thee; thou wilt have a desire to the work of thine hands"* (Job 14: 15).

The call may not be the one you had in mind or planned. It is the call that will place you in the correct and necessary position. *"Who hath saved us, and called us with a holy calling, not according to our works, but according to his purpose and grace, which was given us in Christ Jesus before the world began"* (II Timothy I: 9).

When you are most comfortable and at peace with yourself and those around you, a call may disrupt your well-ordered life. There may be initial resistance. Initial resistance stems from old habits and well-laid-out plans.

The Christ of your being does not take comfort and peace into consideration. A call transcends comfort and peace in this world. Disruption may well be the order of the day. *"Think not that I am come to send peace on earth: I came not to send peace, but a sword"* (Matthew 10: 34).

When you are called, regardless of circumstances, you come to realize the only answer is, "Here am I." *"That the LORD called Samuel: and he answered, Here am I"* (I Samuel 3: 4).

Called is how, as an aware being, you live your life. Fully awakened, you realize your moves and changes on this earth plane were not by accident *or* personal choice. The results of a call may not immediately be realized or even pre-ferred. You live at the beginning, not the end. The present moment is all that exists. There is no time for hesitation. Have you been called?

12

THE
MYSTICAL
SURRENDER

Could you answer the question, "Have you been called?" If you said yes, you are ready for the mystical surrender. Chapters 1 through 11 have given you a window to peek into what the mystical surrendering and following Jesus Christ is all about. A committed mystical surrender, with the practice of the Christ Consciousness Meditation (chapter 15), may allow you to enter through the doorway (your Spiritual Center, chapter 13) and awaken to your spirituality.

For the mystical surrender is to come to the Christ having no expectations and letting go, not giving up but rather giving in. It is saying, "Here I am, Lord, thy will be done." This is followed by rest and trust.

There is nothing to get, nowhere to go. There is only being with what you are with awareness. Mystical surrender is letting go of the idea that you are separate and apart from your God-essence. It wants not to be anywhere else at present.

Surrender is letting go of the false sense of a separate self and resting in the Holy Spirit. You are in complete surrender when loving unconditionally. *"And we have known and believed the love that God hath to us. God is love, and he that dwelleth in love dwelleth in God, and God in him"* (I John 4: 16).

Surrender is not a giving up, but rather a giving in, a giving into that which you are in reality. Surrender is cutting the strings attached to this world. When you let go of everything, you find you already have it all.

Enter into your Spiritual Center. Surrender to the Christ within. Come to Jesus empty and let Him fill you. Trust Christ.

13

YOUR
SPIRITUAL
CENTER

It is in the area of your Spiritual Center that the teaching of the Holy Spirit in the name of Jesus Christ manifests. In mystical surrender to and as a follower of Jesus Christ on this earth plane, your footsteps have but one purpose — to take you to the awareness of the Christ Consciousness, the Oneness of your God being. There exists a spiritual center (it is not an object or feeling you can experience) at the center of the chest between the breasts, referred to as the Spiritual Center.

The Spiritual Center is where the Christ Consciousness is; the prodigal child's (your) home. It is where the Father awaits your arrival and offers the feast of greater awareness of your being. As you are aware of the Spiritual Center area, you may come to realize the Christ Consciousness, where a purer, finer-vibrational energy can be realized. The Spiritual Center is the access door (Jesus) to your reality

It is the Christ in "Christ-ian," through the Spiritual Center, where you may seek to realize your Oneness existence. Your soul and mind, surrendered and devoted to the love of your God, will guide your footsteps into an expanded Spiritual Center. Within the Spiritual Center, the Holy Spirit reveals truth that is manifested through your Christ Consciousness and translated with a purified mind. It is here that all mystical mysteries are resolved. It is here that wisdom is realized. It is here that you may realize your uniqueness.

With a realized awareness of your expanded Spiritual Center, your form may be filled with the light of the Christ and graced with the realization of God's unconditional divine love. Within the Spiritual Center, you are taken on a mystical journey through the Sacred Scriptures along a path traveled by Jesus Christ. It is within the Spiritual Center that you may realize the Christ Consciousness. The Christ Consciousness Meditation may guide you directly to awareness of your Spiritual Center, the Christ Consciousness, and the spirituality of your being. Trust that Jesus is leading the way.

14

THE
CHRIST CONSCIOUSNESS
MEDITATION

The Christ Consciousness Meditation is the "how-to" to access your Spiritual Center. The Oneness of God's essence is to wake you up to Jesus Christ's teaching and your spirituality. The Christ Consciousness Meditation supports, strengthens, and deepens an ongoing relationship with Jesus Christ. It acknowledges and builds upon all previous contemplative teaching, tradition, and biblical reference.

What makes the Christ Consciousness Meditation the pearl of great price, the Holy Grail of silent meditations? It is a revelation - the strait gate and narrow way to the Holy Spirit in the name of Jesus Christ. It is a unique contribution to an inner journey that is a direct path to your inner life with Jesus Christ.

The Christ Consciousness Meditation contains all the realizations that inform and prepare you for an awakened state of consciousness. There are no complicated instructions, rigid rules, or demanding postures. To be so easy and yet so profound in its ability to reveal truth is also its strength. It can only leave you in awe!

Jesus Christ is patient with you at all times, through all of your ups and downs. Now it is your turn. Surrender and trust the Christ of your being is aware precisely where you are and what you need, and moves you along accordingly. *"But he knoweth the way that I take: when he hath tried me, I shall come forth as gold"* (Job 23: 10).

All silent meditations have their value, but they differ. The Christ Consciousness Meditation cuts to the chase. It allows nothing to stand between you and the teaching of the Holy Spirit, in the name of Jesus Christ.

The Christ Consciousness Meditation does not separate your inner practice from your outer practical living.

When practiced with a determined purpose, the fruits of love, joy, peace, goodness, kindness, humility, gentleness, patience, and self-control may express themselves naturally in your daily life. As an individual expression of divine love, these fruits testify to the teaching of Jesus Christ.

Making a change in your routine can be a challenge. You have been taught "to do," and sometimes "overdo." You push, shove, and drive yourself to the brink to get what it is you believe you want. It is always getting and holding on. Effort, effort, all is an effort.

Now you are instructed to do the opposite of what you have been taught: no pushing, no shoving, no holding on, and no driving yourself anywhere. The most significant effort is to show up, surrender, and be patient. Your journey is unique to you.

The Christ Consciousness Meditation is for you who are interested in responding to God without mental or verbal words. In solitude, simplicity, and silence, Jesus Christ guides you through His Holy Spirit to your God spirituality. *"Jesus Christ saith unto him, I am the way, the truth, and the life: no man cometh unto the Father, but by me"* (John 14: 6).

The Christ Consciousness Meditation fulfills Jesus Christ's invitation to, *"Come and find rest for your souls."* With Jesus Christ as a model, scriptures as a reference, tradition as custodian, sacraments as celebration, and selfless service as a mission, the Christ Consciousness Meditation finds its source, sustenance, and direction. The Christ Consciousness Meditation is graced with infinite power and profound rest. It is a subtle, calm inner meditation that allows you to surrender and move effortlessly into your Spiritual Center.

15

THE PRACTICE

As a follower of Jesus, you may walk a spiritual path to the acceptance of Jesus Christ's teaching. The Christ Consciousness Meditation practice carefully responds to Jesus Christ's invitation to *"come"* and painstakingly leads you on a spiritual journey to your all-inclusive Christ presence. The Christ Consciousness Meditation practice presents a simplified version of an ancient tradition. This meditation does not require a sacred word because *you are* the sacred *Word*, the "Word" that existed in the beginning.

"In the beginning was the Word, and the Word was with God, and the Word was God. The same was in the beginning with God. All things were made by him; and without him was not anything made that was made" (John I: 1-3).

The practice is simple and easy. There is no time-prescribed rituals, words, thoughts, sounds, images, or breath. The Christ Consciousness Meditation invites you to rest in the "Word" of who you are, with awareness of your Spiritual Center. *"And the Word was made flesh, and dwelt among us (and we beheld his glory, the glory as of the only begotten of the Father,) full of grace and truth"* (John I: 14).

The Practice:

1. Sit comfortably, rest your hands on your lap or by your sides. Close your eyes, slowly inhale deeply, and slowly exhale. Relax your entire body, and continue to breathe normally.

2. Consciously rest with the awareness of your Spiritual Center *area* (center of the chest, between the breasts).

3. When thoughts or sensations arise, do not dialogue, converse, engage, or respond. Again, return to rest with the awareness of your Spiritual Center *area.*

+++

Is that easy enough? There is no need to complicate the Christ Consciousness Meditation practice. Easy *does* work. The practice takes you directly to your Spiritual Center without any intermediary or mediation. However, you must do the practice.

Hearing, touching, seeing, tasting, and smelling are impressions received through the physical body organs of perception. These sense impressions may draw your immediate attention. Instantly, return to your Spiritual Center *area*.

Practice the silent Christ Consciousness Meditation before a meal and at least two hours after a meal (the changing energy vibration will interfere with the digestion process). Begin the silent meditation for a few minutes and allow it to unfold naturally over time. There is no prescribed length of time required. At the end of a meditation period, take a moment to become consciously aware of your mental and physical senses as they return to normal before resuming your activities.

Remember, you are not trying to make anything happen. You are not seeking to *feel* anything. The mind feels. You are resting with awareness of your Spiritual Center *area* beyond the mind and body states of consciousness.

Be consistent and practice the Christ Consciousness Meditation twice daily. When sitting on a chair, you may wish to use one with armrests for support. Sitting on a cushion on the floor and using a shawl are options. If, for any reason, you find it challenging to become aware of the Spiritual Center *area*, place your hand upon the Spiritual Center area for the first few meditation periods.

You may already have formed the habit of practicing a different meditation. An established habit is not always easy to discontinue, especially if it is of long-standing. A habit is an act of interest often repeated. Replacing one habitual meditation practice with another need not be difficult.

Do not get upset if a previous meditation practice resurfaces and competes with your new practice. To struggle only reinforces the old habit. With loving-kindness, allow the old established meditation practice to rise and treat it as you would any other thought. Do not dialogue. Return to rest with awareness of your Spiritual Center. Gradually, the old practice will no longer rise.

A change in meditation practice is a natural progression on your spiritual walk. Jesus Christ has been waiting for you. He will lovingly welcome the change. Surrender effortlessly, silently, and directly to the awareness of the fullness of your God nature in spirit and truth.

You cannot separate yourself from the Word, which was in the beginning and was made flesh. The Word is made flesh, and it remains the Word of God. The Word of God is the eternal truth. *"Of his own will begat he us with the word of truth, that we should be a kind of firstfruits of his creatures"* (James I: 18).

Without extraneous dialogue, stringent guidelines, or complicated definitions, the Christ Consciousness Meditation practice bypasses potential distractions the mind loves to create. Be faithful, patient, and disciplined in your Christ Consciousness Meditation practice. Judging or evaluating your practice based on your experiences is not wise or helpful.

The fruit of the meditation is always realized in daily life, as the Holy Spirit insinuates itself spontaneously in the name of Jesus Christ. *"But the fruit of the Spirit is love, joy, peace, longsuffering, gentleness, goodness, faith, meekness, temperance: against such, there is no law"* (Galatians 5: 22-23).

The Christ Consciousness Meditation practice invites your participation in the "Word," which provides a means for your primordial "image and likeness" as beloved of God to be realized in its full stature. It may strengthen your surrender. It may support and deepen your relationship with Jesus Christ.

Your chosen path has a particular state of consciousness, be it that of the Buddha, Allah, Krishna, or Christ. You should always practice meditation with the group that supports the state of consciousness of your chosen path. To believe or insist that it will not change the spiritual principle of like consciousness, if you insist on continuing to mix and explore, you are creating an obstacle to finding your way by the "strait gate and narrow way." *"Strive to enter in at the strait gate: for many, I say unto you, will seek to enter in, and shall not be able"* (Luke 13: 24).

As you practice the Christ Consciousness Meditation, you may become aware that the mind finds ways to distract you from becoming aware of your Spiritual Center. The mind is an expert at creating obstacles during a silent meditation practice. Your spoken words, as well as your thoughts, vibrate and go forth. Be faithful to your Christ Consciousness Meditation practice and keep your actions gentle. Think twice before you speak, three times before you act. What you send out by the spoken word, or thought, will undoubtedly "return to sender."

The surrender to Jesus Christ and the flow of your life should be seamless 24/7. There is no time when you are other than a spiritual being. Your daily activities are not separate from your daily silent Christ Consciousness Meditation practice. Your inner guidance is seamless. You may become as aware of Jesus' abiding presence in your practical living as you are during your silent meditation practice. Your life's daily work should not be sequestered from your silent meditation practice. When you open your eyes and get up from your cushion, your meditation does not end.

Practice is the key. Sit for a few minutes twice daily and rest with awareness of your Spiritual Center again and again. Like the prodigal son, you are returning to your Father's house. Jesus Christ awaits your return. With patience, you will find the Christ Consciousness Meditation has a life of its own. Relax, enjoy, and let the meditation *do* you.

16

MINI-EXERCISES

These Mini-Exercises may help your committed surrender along your spiritual journey. They may be utilized whenever necessary. Use them wisely.

1. Listening-In Exercises
The Still Small Voice

It does not matter how many teachers you have followed, courses you have taken, or books you have read. You must become realized. You must wake up to your reality. You must realize God in spirit and truth.

Of course, heaven cannot be taken by force. You may listen-in to your Spiritual Center for guidance. It is all in the Christ Consciousness rising from your Spiritual Center.

As you rest in your Spiritual Center *area* with awareness, the ability to turn a "listening-in" ear into the stirring of the silent voice of God to hear the word of God may increase. In the silence of your

Spiritual Center, the openness and emptiness are rooted in the bedrock of God's abiding presence, divine love. The inner silence may become so deafening that it is loud and clear.

It is from this listening-in posture that you may come to realize the mind of God in spirit and truth. Over time, by listening-in to the inner silence within your Spiritual Center, you may find a silent, sacred language that speaks to you. The silent voice of God may rise.

The Exercise

1. Whenever you have a situation, condition, or question, you may sit quietly with your eyes open or closed. Bring your attention to your Spiritual Center area and quietly listen-in. Listen as though you were waiting for a phone to ring.

2. Allow whatever you are seeking to know to unravel. Allow the thoughts of God's word to rise, and the mind will translate.

As you use the Listening-In Exercise, the inner silence deepens. You may find more clarity of perception in the discernment of conflicting points of view.

Discernment arises with compassion and quickly resolves a present moment's need. Discernment thrives in a listening-in environment that allows your vibrating energy to become calm, balanced, and steady. Be patient. It cannot be rushed. Start with a few minutes as often as you like. You are gradually deepening your inner hearing.

The Listening-in Exercise is different from the Christ Consciousness Meditation in that you are actively listening-in. With Christ Consciousness Meditation practice, you are purely resting with awareness of your Spiritual Center. You are not actively engaged.

If you form the habit of turning within, with a listening-in ear to your Spiritual

Center, you may acquire the inner message at your level of understanding. Your understanding, insights, realizations, and revelations may deepen as you progress on your spiritual journey. When you are prepared and ready to receive, there is not anything that you are denied.

The more you rest in a listening-in mode within your Spiritual Center, the more you may hear. The still, small voice of God is always communicating with you. Listen-in, and you may hear. *"Who hath ears to hear, let him hear"* (Matt. 13: 9).

+++

2. THE NO POWER EXERCISE
Withdraw Your Power

The No Power Exercise is a dialog exercise that may allow you to address a particularly difficult mental issue that repeatedly rises in your mind states of consciousness. This unique dialog exercise is to be used short-term and only when necessary. Its sole purpose is to remove invested power in an emotionally charged situation. It does not replace your twice-daily silent Christ Consciousness Meditation practice. Also, the No Power Exercise should never be mixed with your Christ Consciousness Meditation practice.

Emotional, tormenting rising thoughts are conditioned responses. They may be experienced as a positive or negative solid steel form that seems impenetrable. Because you have previously given the emotionally tormenting rising thoughts power, having accepted a false belief in them, attempting to make the slightest dent may be a considerable struggle. However, that which appears as strong as steel may bend to your will and melt in the furnace of your realization that a conditioned thought has only the power you give it. You are a spiritual being created in the image of your God source.

When practicing, it is most important to remember the immediacy of responding, "NO POWER, GOD IS." The "NO

POWER" is your awareness that the tormenting thought of itself has no power. The "GOD IS" your realization that only God is, and God alone exists in the moment of the tormenting thoughts rising.

The Exercise

1. When a tormenting thought arises, during your daily activities, silently repeat, *"No Power, God Is,"* as often as is necessary.

2. Immediately refocus your attention on the outer activity.

The No Power Exercise may bring you into a neutral zone of non-responding and restore your inner peace. Never use the No Power Exercise while driving or operating any mechanical equipment. Do not exercise or meditate in your parked car, and immediately drive. Always be sure you are fully alert before driving. Whenever your safety is at issue, DO NOT use any form of exercise or meditation.

+++

3. Hand-To-Chest Exercise
Short-Term Solution

The Hand-to-Chest Exercise is to be used during a spiritual energy crisis or time of needed guidance. Conscious awareness transforms. As you surrender to Jesus Christ, many inner changes may occur.

An expansive consciousness may create times of highs and lows. At times, your energy vibrates at such a rapid speed that you may feel as if you are on a roller coaster. Whenever you practice silent meditation, purification may bring change, and an inner struggle may arise when there is resistance to it.

There may be a variety of inner ex- periences that are inexplicable at the time of surrender. The conscious mind state may be struggling to understand the changes that are taking place, which are beyond comprehension. If immediate help is unavailable, the silent Hand-to-Chest Exercise may be a short-term solution. This exercise may be used anywhere and during any activity where your safety is not at risk.

The Exercise

1. When inner vibrating energy turmoil besieges you, or you seek guidance, rest your hand on the area of the Spiritual Center (center of the chest between the breasts).

2. Take a long, deep breath, exhale slowly, relaxing mind and body. Rest your attention on your hand with the silence of awareness. (not on the awareness of your Spiritual Center). If necessary, repeat several times.

The silent Hand-to-Chest Exercise may help bring immediate calm and restore the balance of your vibrating energy. This exercise may be used as needed during any spiritual vibrating-energy crisis or when seeking spiritual guidance. Do not be fooled by the simplicity of this exercise. Many times, Jesus used His hands to heal or to bless. The Hand-to-Chest Exercise may be empowered with the Christ Consciousness of your reality.

+++

4. Temptation Exercise

Temptations want what you have: your God-in-spirit-and-truth realization. Temptations will do just about anything to keep you from your meditation practice. It requires courage to stand up to temptations.

The Temptation Exercise is a silent mental sword that allows you to cut to the quick of temptation at its conceptual stage. Temptations will trample all over your insights, realizations, and revelations. When you are comfortable with your spiritual progress, temptations may rise and come at you in the fiercest ways possible. The further along you are on your spiritual journey, the more intense temptations may become. They will use any means and seem to have a life of their own.

Being on a spiritual journey is an invitation for temptations to rise. The more you resist, the stronger and more insistent the temptations become. They feed on your strength. Temptations never desist. Right up to your passing, a temptation will rise to play with your mind. *"And at the ninth hour, Jesus cried with a loud voice, saying, El-o-i, El-o-i, la-ma sa-bach tha-ni? Which is, being interpreted, "My God, my God, why hast thou forsaken me?"* (Mark 15: 34).

Don't be fooled by what temptations may present. They may come at you with very appealing offers. It is the work of temptations to make you an offer you can't refuse.

There are many of you who, like the parable of the seed, which was the word of God, fall prey easily to temptation. Power, once grounded in truth, gives you the upper hand. You can refuse temptation's offer and grow stronger with your awareness of temptations.

Temptations are seducers that invite you to betray your reality. Strive to be more like the seed that fell upon the good ground. It does not matter if a temptation appears as a person, situation, friend, or foe; the Temptation Exercise is the same.

The Exercise

1. Always stay alert to the possibilities of a rising temptation.

2. When a temptation arises, silently, mentally say, "GET YE BEHIND ME, SATAN." Silently, mentally repeat the phrase as often as the temptation rises. Do not engage in dialogue or mentally engage with the rising temptation. A temptation thrives on chatter.

17

SUPPORTERS AND TOOLS
Helpful Suggestions

The following are a few helpful suggestions for your meditation practice. Work with the ones that are most comfortable for your practice.

1. SITTING

Sitting is the usual position taken during a silent meditation practice. Sitting may be on a comfortable couch, chair, or on the floor. If you practice sitting on a chair, you may choose to use an armchair for safety. Keep your head and chin relaxed and your hands on your lap. Sit, wearing loose clothing.

Sitting in the same area of your home or place of practice may help you feel more comfortable with your practice. However, the practice may be done anywhere where your safety is not at risk. Sit still during your practice. If discomfort rises, slowly and quietly adjust your posture. Any movement while practicing should be performed in very slow motion.

The less you disturb your vibrating energy, the better.

If you wish to stop your practice, stop. Do not force yourself to practice for any particular length of time. Allow the time you practice to increase naturally. Be patient and gentle with your silent practice. Your determined purpose of sitting will form the sitting habit and allow you to practice more easily.

If, for health reasons, you cannot sit, then, of course, lie down. However, guard against falling asleep. Remember, a fool goes to sleep, and a fool wakes up. You are practicing a silent meditation to wake up to your reality, not to take a nap. Give yourself a moment to readjust to your immediate environment at the end of your practice. Always get up carefully and slowly from your practicing position.

2. TOOLS:

Tools are aids on your spiritual path that can assist you. Books, tapes, teachings, stories, symbols, and rituals are tools. Those are some of the many tools of various kinds. What is considered sacred to you may not be to another. You may respect all available tools; it is your belief in any particular tool that matters.

A shawl is a tool that you may wish to use. It may allow you to turn more easily. Tools should be approached with contemplative reverence. However, tools are *about* truth, *not* truth itself. The truth is who and what you are. It is not outside of your reality.

Use whatever tool/s you are drawn to and believe may help. However, guard against becoming attached to any tool. If you have taken a boat to cross a river, once there, you do not carry the boat on your head. You leave it for someone else to use. Be grateful for its use; then leave it behind when you finish with any tool and move on.

The critical thing to remember is that you never use any tool when you are doing your silent meditation practice. Mixing your practice with any tool or other practice will stall your progress. Don't do it. Your inner guidance needs no tool and can teach you all things directly. All tools serve to help you to progress. Some may be of greater or lesser use at different stages of your meditation practice.

3. FLEXIBILITY

Flexibility allows you to adjust, correct, reconsider, and change. You may find flexibility difficult when you begin a new silent meditation practice. You may have been taught to be consistent with your practice time and place. However, that may not always be possible.

Once your time and place are established, even a temporary change may be resisted. An active lifestyle may require flexibility at any time. Be prepared to adjust to new surroundings and accept the changes as they may occur.

There are times when you must adjust to a new routine. Being flexible will allow you to adapt your practice whenever and wherever necessary. Do not sacrifice your practice in the fires of temptation.

If you are not flexible, traveling for a time to a strange environment could cause an interruption of your practice. Do not trouble yourself with the outer appearances of change in your life. All too often, you may become attached to a particular time, place, or sitting cushion. You want everything to be the same—nothing out of order. In most situations, that would be ideal. As a dedicated truth-seeker, you must be flexible enough to adjust to a moment of change as it presents itself.

The Christ Consciousness Meditation practice is a direct path to your

Spiritual Center and revealed truth. However, you are never locked into a rigid position on the path. Spiritual growth causes changes and requires flexibility to adjust and accept changes as they occur.

4. TIME

Time is relative to this earth's plane of opposites. When you begin a silent meditation practice, you start with a minute twice daily. It is not necessary to intentionally place strict time limits on your silent practice. Allow your practice to expand itself.

This allows your mind and body to adjust to sitting naturally. You do not want to judge your practice periods by length. Longer is not better or shorter worse. The critical issue is to do the practice twice a day. One minute is an eternity with the silence of awareness.

Your sitting will eventually become a habit. The time necessary for your practice will become established and comfortable. There never is a need to force your practice time. If you are restless or uncomfortable, get up and return to the practice at another time when you are at ease.

~~

The fruit of your practice will be experienced in your daily life as you can respond to the needs of others and your own legitimate needs. A silent meditation practice time need not be dreaded, nor should it be forced. Your practice will meet your needs in its own time. Relax and let the practice do you. Time, place, cushions, and shawls are valuable tools, but all you ever need to practice the Christ Consciousness Meditation is you.

CONCLUSION

"AND THIS IS life eternal, that they might know thee the only true God, and Jesus Christ, whom thou hast sent" (John 17: 3).

You may mistakenly believe you must die before realizing your reality. Truth exists within you now, and you may enter into the realization of it. Your spirituality is not a myth. It is real now. There is not any time that your reality cannot be realized.

No one can take you there. No one can give it to you. No one can take it away from you. No one can deny your entrance. No one can steal it from you. No one can buy it for you. No one can sell it to you, and no one can surrender for you.

With the Christ Consciousness Meditation, you may become consciously aware of who you are. This realization is always yours, free and clear. Mystery or symbolic rituals need not surround your reality's availability. The silent Christ Consciousness Meditation is a path that may take you directly to your spirituality within your Spiritual Center.

Come home to the source of your being without ever taking one step in any direction. The Christ Consciousness Meditation brings a greater dimension to your daily practical outer living. You do not have to travel, pay large sums of money, perform mysterious rituals, or undergo difficult initiations. Turn within, and you are there, where you never left and will always be. Turn within to the presence and reality of the kingdom of God.

The silent Christ Consciousness Meditation may help you turn within. Your kingdom is not of this world. Your peace beyond understanding is not of this world. Your eternal life is not of this world. The reality of your life is knocking at the inner door of your Spiritual Center.

Surrender and turn within, turn within. *"Behold, I stand at the door and knock: if any man hears my voice and opens the door, I will come into him and will sup with him, and he with me"* (Revelation 3: 20). Jesus is knocking at the inner door of your Spiritual Center, won't you open it?

You are Heaven and

Earth

and all things in

between.

You are a Moment now

seen and unseen.

TRANSLATOR

Carla R. Mancari is an author, translator, life guide, and teacher. She seeks to improve the self-confidence and self-esteem of individuals from all walks of life so that they can meet life's challenges. For more than 45 years, she has guided individuals in understanding life's spiritual principles, activities, and rising emotions in their private and daily lives. Carla is the recipient of the Christ Consciousness Meditation and the Minute Meditation. Although she had never attended high school and was labeled a retarded child, she attained two University degrees: a B.A. from the University of South Carolina in Columbia, South Carolina, and an MEd from South Carolina State University in Orangeburg, South Carolina. Carla studied at Brigham Young University and attended the School of the Americas in Switzerland.

Carla led a class action lawsuit in the United States Supreme Court to protect minorities' rights (Morton v. Mancari, 1973) and was a certified psychologist.

She served in the United States Air Force. Traveling worldwide for many years, Carla studied with Christian, Hindu, and Buddhist masters. She was a guest on the Larry King Radio Show and a guest lecturer at various colleges, professional groups, book clubs, and at book signings. Carla gained national recognition when featured in *Good Housekeeping*, "The Education of Carla Mancari, 1969." It chronicled her life in 1967-68 when she was the first white woman to receive a Master's degree from the all-Black South Carolina State College in Orangeburg, South Carolina. She is the author of many books. Carla's greatest joy is helping individuals realize their self-worth, unique gifts/talents, and full potential, and wake up to their spiritual reality.

BOOKS

Mancari, Carla R., *The Lessons: How to Understand Spiritual Principles, Spiritual Activities and Rising Emotions, A Comprehensive Collection.* Celestial Literary Group, 2026.

- - - *Christ Consciousness Meditation Practice: Pocket Size.* Celestial Literary Group, 2026.

- - - *Loneliness.* Celestial Literary Group, 2026.

- - - *Racism, Antisemitism+: A Disease of the Mind.* Celestial Literary Group, 2026.

- - - *The Christ Consciousness Meditation Teaching Guide.* Celestial Literary Group, 2026.

- - - *Metaphysical Questions with Answers from the Christ Consciousness.* Celestial Literary Group, 2026.

- - - *When Jesus Is the Guru: A Wayward Christian's Spiritual Walk.* Celestial Literary Group, 2010.

- - - *Eco-You: A Power of One, Improve Your Health, Improve Your Life.* Celestial Literary Group, 2019.

- - - *Walking on the Grass: A White Woman In A Black World.* Celestial Literary Group, 2016.

- - - *Abortion and The Bible: The Abortion Dilemma: A Scriptural Response, A Woman's Spirituality.* Celestial Literary Group, 2017.

- - - *Racism: The Pain of Invisibility.* Celestial Literary Group, 2017.

- - - *The Rising Emotions: Understanding and Mastering Them.* Celestial Literary Group, 2017.

- - - *The Mystical Path: The Serious Student.* Celestial Literary Group, 2017.

- - - *Spiritual Principles: Understanding, Realizing, and Living Them.* Celestial Literary Group, 2018.

- - - *Climate Change: Consciousness Change.* Celestial Literary Group, 2017.

- - - *Words: Locks On The Door or Keys To The Kingdom.* Celestial Literary Group, 2018.

- - - *Aging: Physical to the Mystical.* Celestial Literary Group, 2018.

- - - *Divine Love: Your Nature.* Celestial Literary Group, 2018.

- - - *The Lazarus Rising: The Kundalini – A Rising Dormant Energy.* Celestial Literary Group, 2018.

- - - *Depression: Hopelessness – A Disconnection.* Celestial Literary Group, 2018.

- - - *Jesus Christ: Teacher.* Celestial Literary Group, 2018.

- - - *The Mystical Surrender: Giving In.* Celestial Literary Group, 2018.

- - - *Death Ain't Dead: Empty Graves.* Celestial Literary Group, 2018.

- - - *Common Decency: Your DNA.* Celestial Literary Group, 2018.

- - - *Christians?: Common Decency.* Celestial Literary Group, 2018.

- - - *Beyond Buddhism: Meditations.* Celestial Literary Group, 2018.

- - - *Exit: Get Ready, Set, Go.* Celestial Literary Group, 2018.

- - - *Meditation: Good For You.* Celestial Literary Group, 2018.

- - - *How To Love "You": Begins with You.* Celestial Literary Group, 2018.

- - - *Consciousness: Yours.* Celestial Literary Group, 2018.

- - - *Suicide: Understanding It.* Celestial Literary Group, 2018.

- - - *Detachment: Realizations.* Celestial Literary Group, 2018.

- - - *Detachment: Christian.* Celestial Literary Group, 2018.

- - - *Sexual Abuse By The Church – Its Root, Coerced Celibacy.* Celestial Literary Group, 2018.

- - - *Guns and Guts: The Courage To Act.* Celestial Literary Group, 2018.

- - - *Jesus, The Way: A Mystical Understanding.* Celestial Literary Group, 2019.

- - - *Motivation: Self-Motivated.* Celestial Literary Group, 2019.

- - - *Totally Free: Is Killing Me.* Celestial Literary, Group, 2018.

- - - *A 30-Second Meditation For Teenagers.* Celestial Literary Group, 2018.

- - - *A 30-Second Meditation For Seniors.* Celestial Literary Group, 2017.

- - - *The Five Faces Of Love. Celestial Literary Group, 2019.*

- - - *Angel In The House.* Celestial Literary Group, 2019 (A Children's Book).

- - - *Put It In The Bible: Prayerful Requests.* Celestial Literary Group, 2019.

- - - *Hate: A Dark Emotion.* Celestial Literary Group, 2019.

- - - *Greed: It's Addictive.* Celestial Literary Group, 2019.

- - - *On Being Young: Choices.* Celestial Literary Group, 2019.

- - - *Gratitude: Expressed, Sincere.* Celestial Literary Group, 2019.

- - - *Humor: A Necessity.* Celestial Literary Group, 2019.

- - - *A Christian: Are You One?* Celestial Literary Group, 2019.

- - - *Habit: How To Switch Meditation Practices.* Celestial Literary Group, 2019.

- - - *Impeachment: Living On The Dark Side.* Celestial Literary Group, 2019.

- - - *The Jesus I Know.* Celestial Literary Group, 2019.

- - - *Grace: Spirit And Truth.* Celestial Literary Group, 2019.

- - - *Temptation.* Celestial Literary Group, 2019.

- - - *The Christian Journey: Teacher Student Relationship.* Celestial Literary Group, 2019.

- - - *The Beloved: Who Is The Beloved?* Celestial Literary Group, 2019.

- - - *What Now, Lord? Enlightenment.* Celestial Literary Group, 2019.

- - - *What If I Were Gay?* Celestial Literary Group, 2019.

- - - *Mother Mary: Mother of Jesus.* Celestial Literary Group, 2019.

- - - *I Remember America.* Celestial Literary Group, 2019.

- - - *The Overcoming: Jesus.* Celestial Literary Group, 2019.

- - - *When Faith Is Not Enough.* Celestial Literary Group, 2019.

- - - *The Plane of Opposites: The Work.* Celestial Literary Group, 2020.

- - - *Crisis.* Celestial Literary Group, 2020.

- - - *Grief: Gut-Wrenching Emotion.* Celestial Literary Group, 2020.

- - - *God.* Celestial Literary Group, 2020.

- - - *Regrets: Do You Have Any?* Celestial Literary Group, 2020.

- - - *1968, 1968,1968: The Mind of A Racist.* Celestial Literary Group, 2020.

- - - *Satan.* Celestial Literary Group, 2020.

- - - *Practice Practice: Meditation.* Celestial Literary Group, 2021.

- - - *Christians Without Jesus: Prodigal Son's Journey.* Celestial Literary Group, 2021.

- - - *From Here To There.* Celestial Literary Group, 2021.

- - - *An Awakening Path: Christian Spiritual Principles.* Celestial Literary Group, 2021.

- - - *Holy Scriptures: Uplifting, Inspiring and Comforting.* Celestial Literary Group, 2021.

- - - *Male Female: The Split Soul.* Celestial Literary Group, 2021.

- - - *The Inner Message: Theological Mystical State.* Celestial Literary Group, 2021.

- - - *A Guide To Understanding Mind's Contents And Realizations.* Celestial Literary Group, 2021.

- - - *A Sister's Laughter: Oh! How I Miss It* Celestial Literary Group, 2021.

- - - *Churches: Are They Necessary?* Celestial Literary Group, 2021.

- - - *Metaphysical: Stories and Poems.* Celestial Literary Group, 2021.

- - - *Jesus, Jesus, Jesus.* Celestial Literary Group, 2021.

- - - *The Disciple and The Mystical Guide.* Celestial Literary Group, 2021.

- - - *The Holy Trinity: 1+1+1=1, No Mystery.* Celestial Literary Group, 2021.

- - - *Fear of Jesus: Why?.* Celestial Literary Group, 2021.

- - - *Symbols and Rituals: Christian.* Celestial Literary Group, 2021.

- - - *Christian Minute Meditation.* Celestial Literary Group, 2021.

- - - *Sin!.* Celestial Literary Group, 2021.

- - - *Compassion.* Celestial Literary Group, 2021.

- - - *Silence.* Celestial Literary Group, 2021.

- - - *The Spiritual Zone.* Celestial Literary Group, 2022.

- - - *The Bible Scriptures: Mystical Understanding.* Celestial Literary Group, 2022.

- - - *Lead Us Not Into Temptation: The Lord's Prayer.* Celestial Literary Group, 2022.

- - - *Let's Talk About Jesus, Or Not.* Celestial Literary Group, 2022.

- - - *For The Love of Jesus: Come Back To Your Church.* Celestial Literary Group, 2022.

- - - *Abortion, When Life Does Not Begin! Exodus 21:22-25.* Celestial Literary Group, 2022.

- - - *Morton vs. Mancari: A Plaintiff's Response: How An Average Joe (woman) Landed In The US Supreme Court.* Celestial Literary Group, 2022.

- - - *Christian Spiritual Exercises: The Inner Journey.* Celestial Literary Group, 2023.

- - - *The Kingdom Of God – A Gift.* Celestial Literary Group, 2023.

- - - *An Expression of Love.* Celestial Literary Group, 2023.

- - - *Choices and Decisions On a Spiritual Journey.* Celestial Literary Group, 2024.

- - - *Love Your Enemies: How Can You Do That?.* Celestial Literary Group, 2024.

- - - *Outer Space and Inner Space Travel.* Celestial Literary Group, 2024.

- - - *God – Love: Poets Write About It.* Celestial Literary Group, 2024.

- - - *The Still Small Voice, You Can Hear It.* Celestial Literary Group, 2024.

- - - *The Resurrection: Rising Beyond Body Consciousness.* Celestial Literary Group, 2024.

- - - *Sexual Spiritual Intercourse: Oneness.* Celestial Literary Group, 2024.

- - - *Child Of God: In Spirit and Truth.* Celestial Literary Group, 2024.

- - - *"My Child," Blessed Mother Mary's.* Celestial Literary Group, 2024.

- - - *Strait Gate and Narrow Way: "Few There Be That Find It".* Celestial Literary Group, 2024.

- - - *Strait Gate and Narrow Way: "Few There Be That Find It", Pocket Size.* Celestial Literary Group, 2024.

- - - *The End Of The Beginning, Our Spiritual Journey.* Celestial Literary Group, 2024.

- - - *A Cat Story.* Celestial Literary Group, 2025.

Mancari, Carla. R. *and* **Carpenter, Mary B.** *Scriptural Reference For - The Lessons, A Comprehensive Collection.* Celestial Literary Group, 2026.

- - -*The Minute Meditation, Book 1: It Is Profound!* Celestial Literary Group, 2022.

- - -*The Minute Meditation, Book 2: Workbook, It Is Profound!.* The Celestial Literary Group, 2022.

- - - *The Minute Meditation, It Is Profound! Book 3: The Essentials.* Celestial Literary Group, 2022.

- - - *The Minute Meditation, It Is Profound! Book 4: A Diet For The Soul.* Celestial Literary Group, 2022.

- - - *The Minute Meditation, It Is Profound! Book 5: The Three of You, You Are Never Alone.* Celestial Literary Group, 2022.

- - - *The Minute Meditation, It Is Profound! Book 6: Pocket Size.* Celestial Literary Group, 2022.

- - - *The Minute Meditation, It Is Profound! Book 7 – Teaching Guide.* Celestial Literary Group, 2022.

- - - *The Minute Meditation, It Is Profound! Book 8 – The 4th Chakra.* Celestial Literary Group, 2026.

- - - *Spirituality: Yours.* Celestial Literary Group, 2021.

- - - *Dreams: States of Consciousness.* Celestial Literary Group, 2021.

- - - *A Christian Service With A Silent Christian Meditation.* Celestial Literary Group, 2024.

Casey-Martus, Sandra, and Mancari, Carla R. *The Lessons, How to Understand Spiritual Principles, Spiritual Activities and Rising Emotions, Lessons with Stories Along a Spiritual Journey.* Celestial Literary Group, 2026.

NOTES